I0480145

# 100 Character Prompts

## 2020 Edition

Written by Jaz Johnson

Edited by Jaz Johnson & Brandon Tate

Formatted by Jaz Johnson

Cover Design by Jaz Johnson

Copyright © 2020 by TC Studios LLC

First paperback edition published January 1st, 2020.

ISBN: 978-1-951626-06-8 (e-book)

ISBN: 978-1-951626-07-5 (paperback)

Published by TC Studios LLC

www.TCStudiosHQ.com

**Table of Contents**

## Introductions

Hello! Welcome to our 2020 edition of *100 Character Prompts*. This book is a part of our creative group, **Prompt Party**. It's going to get your creative mojo flowing and make you want to start drawing!

This book includes the following:

1. 100 prompts in eight different mediums (a), eight different genres (b), and ten different themes (c).
   a. Pencil (P), Color Pencil (CP), Acrylic Paint (AP), Marker (M), Crayon (C), Gouache (G), Watercolor (W), and Ink (I).
   b. Fantasy (F), Science Fiction (SF), Romance (R), Horror (H), Dystopian (D), Slice of Life (SL), Action & Adventure (AA), and Mystery (M).
   c. Body Type, Characteristics, Hobbies, Race & Ethnicity, Modifications, Occupations, Personalities, Negative Traits, Aesthetics, and Features.
2. 10 drawing exercises – one for each theme.
3. 10 writing exercises – one for each theme.

## How To Use Our Prompts

Each prompt will list a hypothetical situation and a few suggested mediums to draw with, as well as suggested paths you can take with the prompt. You are **not** required to draw in with mediums or use the brainstorming sections. They are **only suggestions**.

Some prompts talk about you, but you don't always have to draw/write yourself. You can make up a character, or characters, too!

The goal is to draw or write a piece of work using the prompts provided. How you get there is ultimately up to you.

## Share Your Work & Tag Us

We would love to be able to see the amazing things you come up with and tell you how much we love them.

To do that, all you have to do is post your work to Facebook, Instagram or Twitter and tag us @PromptParty. Then we'll be able to see, share, and comment on them!

## Submit To Our Anthologies

Would you like your work to be published? People are using our prompt books across the country, and many of them are submitting their work to our annual anthologies.

An anthology is a collection of work by many different people. Each year, we publish several with work made using our various prompt books.

The authors and artists of the published submissions receive 25% royalties (must be 18+), and 10% goes back into helping communities like yours. This money goes towards public school donations, public library donations, and more. So, help your community out by getting more people involved!

For more details on royalties and our mission to give back to communities across the country, visit our website, www.TCStudiosHQ.com.

To submit your work to our anthology, please do the following:

- Send an email to submissions@tcstudioshq.com with the following:
  - **Subject Line:**
    - 100 Character Prompts Anthology Submission (2020)
  - **Body:**
    - First and last name (or pen/artist name).
    - The genre/medium you used.
  - **Attachments:**
    - Attached work.
      - Attached as a **PDF** for literature.
      - Attached as a **PNG** for art.
    - Attached signed publication form.
      - You can find this on our website.

If you are selected, we will reach out to you to request more information.

For more information on our other anthologies and an in-depth guide on how to submit to them, visit our website, www.TCStuidiosHQ.com.

## Check Out Our Work

Did you know that we also publish novels, comics, and other creative guides?

To find out more about everything we publish and where you can read/get them, visit our website, www.TCStudiosHQ.com.

# Chapter One: Body Type.

#1 – Curvy. (M) (F) | (P) (AP) (W)

---

*Brainstorm (Writing) ...*

- How do curves affect this person?
  - How might someone's curves aid what they're trying to accomplish?
    - How might it hinder them?

---

*Brainstorm (Drawing) ...*

- Focus on: Body Language.
  - How can you position the body to emphasize and highlight this character's curves?

---

**Writing Exercise #1**

Write about the transition of weight gain/loss.

---

7

#2 – Straight & Narrow. (AA) (SF) | (M) (G) (CP)

---

*Brainstorm (Writing) ...*

- Is this person agile?
    - Does this aid them with speed?
- Are they self-conscious about their body? Are they confident?
- How might it relate to their personality?
    - Are they also on the "straight & narrow"?

---

*Brainstorm (Drawing) ...*

- Life Study.
    - Go out and find a person with this prompt to sketch.
    - See if someone you know will let you draw them!

---

**You can share your work with us on Facebook, Instagram & Twitter!**

Tag us @PromptParty and use #PromptParty.

We'd love to see what you come up with!

#3 – Thick. (R) (SL) | (I) (C) (P)

---

*Brainstorm (Writing)* ...

- Is this their natural body weight/type?
    - Is there a story behind their weight?
- Does their thickness translate into physical strength?
    - Do they use this strength often?

---

*Brainstorm (Drawing)* ...

- Challenge: Monochrome.
    - Try drawing this scene using only one gradient of color.

---

**Do you want your work published?**

You can submit any work made using our prompts to our annual anthologies! Published submissions receive shared 25% royalties.

You can find more information on our website, www.TCStudiosHQ.com.

#4 – Short & Stumpy. (AA) (D) | (W) (M) (C)

---

*Brainstorm (Writing) ...*

- How does their body type tie into their personality?
    - Do tall people annoy them?
    - Is movement difficult?

---

*Brainstorm (Drawing) ...*

- Practice different types of shading techniques.
    - Hatching.
    - Cross-Hatching.
    - Stippling.
    - Scribbling.
    - Contour Lines.

---

**Did you know?**

A percentage of every anthology sold goes towards helping communities like yours. This includes donations to charities, funding of scholarships, creating of programs, and more!

You can find more information on our website, www.TCStudiosHQ.com.

#5 – Muscular. (H) (SF) | (AP) (CP) (I)

---

*Brainstorm (Writing)* ...

- Are they proud of their body?
    - What kind of work/discipline went into creating it?
    - Is there a story behind why they worked so hard?
- What is their profession?
    - Is a muscular body needed?

---

*Brainstorm (Drawing)* ...

- Life Study.
    - Go out and find a person with this prompt to sketch.
    - See if someone you know will let you draw them!

---

**Did you know?**

In addition to our annual prompt anthologies, every year we have themed anthologies that you can also submit to!

You can find more information on our website, www.TCStudiosHQ.com.

#6 – Well-toned. (M) (F) | (P) (G) (W)

---

*Brainstorm (Writing) ...*

- Describe the structure of this character's body in your work.
    o What attributes does it have when it moves?
- Maybe write about this character dancing or doing something with continuous motion.

---

*Brainstorm (Drawing) ...*

- Experiment: Colored Lighting.
    o When/if you are applying lighting effects to this piece, try using a different color instead of just a lighter gradient of the lit area.

---

**Drawing Exercise #1**

Draw 10 different body types in a line-up.

---

12

#7 – Slender. (AA) (H) | (M) (I) (C)

---

*Brainstorm (Writing)* ...

- How might their clothing highlight their slenderness?
- How might lighting and shadows affect this person's body type?
    - Is it sharper?
        - If so, where?
- Are their facial features sharper?
    - How might you go about describing them?

---

*Brainstorm (Drawing)* ...

- Practice: Hair.
    - Study the flow and lighting dimensions of hair and implement the techniques into your drawing.

**Looking for a challenge?**

Try doing one of our prompts with your friend(s)! See if you can come up with something together.

#8 – Chunky. (SF) (R) | (CP) (W) (P)

---

*Brainstorm (Writing) ...*

- How might you describe this body type without using the prompt word?
    - Play around with how you can create imagery in the description portion of your work.

---

*Brainstorm (Drawing) ...*

- Practice: Skin Tones.
    - Study skin tone palettes and techniques and implement them in your drawing.

---

**Did you know?**

We also make books to help with storytelling. With help on things like creating characters, world-building, magic systems, and more!

You can find more information on our website, www.TCStudiosHQ.com.

#9 – Broad. (F) (M) | (G) (AP) (M)

---

*Brainstorm (Writing)* ...

- What kind of clothing could emphasis this feature?
  - A suit?
- What part of this person is broad?
  - Their shoulders?
  - Their nose?
  - Their chest?

---

*Brainstorm (Drawing)* ...

- Challenge: No Linework.
  - Try drawing this scene with no outlining – just dive right in with blocks of color!

---

**Did you know?**

We also publish novels and comics that you can read!

You can find more information on our website, www.TCStudiosHQ.com.

#10 – Bulky. (D) (SF) | (I) (P) (CP)

---

*Brainstorm (Writing) ...*

- What could this mean?
    - Muscular?
    - Tall and broad?
- Play around with how this could translate into this character's figure.

---

*Brainstorm (Drawing) ...*

- Challenge: Opposite Colors.
    - Pick a color and it's opposite (ex: red and green).
    - Try coloring this piece with only those two colors and their gradients.

---

**Do you want to give us a prompt for next year's edition?**

You can submit prompt ideas you have based on next year's chapter themes. Credit will be given if selected.

You can find more information on our website, www.TCStudiosHQ.com.

# Chapter Two: Characteristics.

#11 – Hot-headed. (AA) (F) (SL) | (CP) (I) (M)

---

*Brainstorm (Writing)* ...

- What happens when this person loses their temper?
    o How to people around them react?
- Are they aware of this trait?
    o Are they doing anything to manage it?

---

*Brainstorm (Drawing)* ...

- Experiment: Comic Strip.
    o Try drawing this as a short comic strip.

---

**Writing Exercise #2**

Write a character with a split personality – and explore the characteristics of all of them.

#12 – Sneaky. (SF) (M) (D) | (G) (P) (AP)

---

*Brainstorm (Writing)* ...

- Why is this character being sneaky?
  - What are they trying to accomplish?
  - Is there a goal?
    - Are they just sneaky to be sneaky?
- Describe what their actions/thoughts are like.

---

*Brainstorm (Drawing)* ...

- Focus on: Background.
  - Tell the story with the use of the background and its environment. Think about the use and placement of specific items to help get the point across.

---

**Did you know?**

We post daily writing & drawing prompts on our Social Medias for everyone to participate in.

Find us @PromptParty and use #PromptParty.

You can find more information on our website, www.TCStudiosHQ.com.

#13 – Loving. (R) (H) (M) | (C) (I) (W)

---

*Brainstorm (Writing) ...*

- How does this character show their loving nature?
  - What are some things they do?
  - What are some things they say?
- How do other people view them?
- How to they view other people?

---

*Brainstorm (Drawing) ...*

- Challenge: Monochrome.
  - Try drawing this scene using only one gradient of color.

---

**Did you know?**

In addition to posting daily on Social Media, we have daily interactive posts on our YouTube channel, Podcast, and Blog.

You can find more information on our website, www.TCStudiosHQ.com.

#14 – Magical. (AA) (SL) (F) | (CP) (G) (M)

---

*Brainstorm (Writing)* ...

- What is magical about this person?
    - Are they extremely lucky?
    - Are they actually magical?
- What do they do with their magic?

---

*Brainstorm (Drawing)* ...

- Practice: Hands.
    - Study up on some hand techniques and implement them in your drawing.
        - Maybe they're casting a spell, or holding a scroll, or waving their wand.

---

**Remember!**

The listed genres/mediums and brainstorming boxes are **only suggestions!** We encourage you to do/use whatever you want.

#15 – Nosey. (R) (M) (D) | (AP) (M) (P)

---

*Brainstorm (Writing)* ...

- What is this character being nosey about?
- Are they eavesdropping on someone?
    - Spying?
    - Social Media stalking?

---

*Brainstorm (Drawing)* ...

- Experiment: Bold Line Work.
    - When you've finished lining your work (if you're lining), try making some areas thicker than others.
        - It can be dramatically, or just a bit.
            - Take note of how it changes the tone of your work.

---

**Be The First To Know.**

Join our newsletter and be the first to know about new prompt books, novels, comics, giveaways, freebies, coupons, and anything else we've got going on!

Find our newsletter on our website, www.TCStudiosHQ.com.

#16 – Noisy. (SF) (H) (F) | (I) (CP) (W)

---

*Brainstorm (Writing) ...*

- Who is making so much noise?
    - Why?
    - How?

---

*Brainstorm (Drawing) ...*

- Challenge: No references.
    - Put your muscle memory to the test and draw this scene without using any references.
        - Good luck!

---

**Drawing Exercise #2**

Draw 10 different facial expressions that are tied to different characteristics.

---

#17 – Cowardly. (AA) (H) (R) | (C) (P) (G)

---

*Brainstorm (Writing)* ...

- Why is this person so scared?
  - What are they scared of?
  - Is it reasonable?
  - Did something happen to them to provoke the fear?

---

*Brainstorm (Drawing)* ...

- Focus on: Body Language.
  - How can you position the body to emphasize and highlight this character's fear?

---

**You can share your work with us on Facebook, Instagram & Twitter!**

Tag us @PromptParty and use #PromptParty.

We'd love to see what you come up with!

#18 – Heroic. (AA) (M) (D) | (AP) (W) (CP)

---

*Brainstorm (Writing) ...*

- What has this character done that's heroic?
  - What did it entail?
  - How do they feel about it?
  - If others know, how do they feel about it?

---

*Brainstorm (Drawing) ...*

- Challenge: Continuous line.
  - Try drawing this scene with one continuous line.
  - You can color the finished image.

---

**Do you want your work published?**

You can submit any work made using our prompts to our annual anthologies! Published submissions receive shared 25% royalties.

You can find more information on our website, www.TCStudiosHQ.com.

#19 – Flirtatious. (R) (SL) (F) | (M) (I) (P)

---

*Brainstorm (Writing)* ...

- Who is this character flirtatious with?
  - Is it with anyone?
- What do they do when they're flirting?
  - Are there any specific mannerisms or actions?

---

*Brainstorm (Drawing)* ...

- Experiment: Exaggerated Proportions/Features.
  - Get a little cartoony.
  - How might exaggerating certain features help the imagery?

**Did you know?**

A percentage of every anthology sold goes towards helping communities like yours. This includes donations to charities, funding of scholarships, creating of programs, and more!

You can find more information on our website, www.TCStudiosHQ.com.

#20 – Shy. (SF) (SL) (H) | (G) (AP) (W)

---

*Brainstorm (Writing)* ...

- What is this character shy about?
    - Is it something specific?
    - Why are they shy about it?
- Are they just generally a shy person?

---

*Brainstorm (Drawing)* ...

- Play around with your shading techniques.
    - How can you emphasize the tension or the comic relief of the scene using shading and lighting?

---

**Did you know?**

In addition to our annual prompt anthologies, every year we have themed anthologies that you can also submit to!

You can find more information on our website, www.TCStudiosHQ.com.

# Chapter Three: Hobbies.

#21 – Violin. (SL) (M) | (CP) (M) (I)

*Brainstorm (Writing)* ...

- What are they doing with the violin?
  - Practicing?
  - Performing?
  - Cleaning it?
- If they are playing, what song is being played?
  - Are they skilled, or a beginner?

*Brainstorm (Drawing)* ...

- Challenge: Color Palette.
  - Use a random color palette generator or ask a friend to pick 3-5 colors for you to use.

**Writing Exercise #3**

Write out your process for partaking in your favorite hobby – in story format.

#22 – Painting/Drawing. (R) (D) | (AP) (G) (C)

---

*Brainstorm (Writing)* ...

- What is being painted/drawn?
- What medium is being used?
- What is it being made on?
    - Canvas?
    - Paper?
    - Computer program?

---

*Brainstorm (Drawing)* ...

- Practice: Lighting.
    - Study color choice, gradients, and placement techniques of lighting and implement them in your drawing.

---

**Looking for a challenge?**

Try doing one of our prompts with your friend(s)! See if you can come up with something together.

#23 – Photography. (H) (SF) | (W) (M) (P)

---

*Brainstorm (Writing)* ...

- What kind of camera is being used?
- What is the lighting like?
- What is being photographed?
  - Is it for a specific purpose?

---

*Brainstorm (Drawing)* ...

- Practice: Anatomy.
  - Study proportions, positioning, and structure techniques and implement them in your drawing.

---

**Did you know?**

We also make books to help with storytelling. With help on things like creating characters, world-building, magic systems, and more!

You can find more information on our website, www.TCStudiosHQ.com.

#24 – Knitting. (SL) (D) | (I) (C) (AP)

---

*Brainstorm (Writing)* ...

- What are they knitting?
  - Are they doing it well?
  - How far along it is?
  - What color(s) is/are being used?
  - What/who is it for?

---

*Brainstorm (Drawing)* ...

- Experiment: Exaggerated Proportions/Features.
  - Get a little cartoony.
  - How might exaggerating certain features relate to the story behind the image?

---

**Did you know?**

We also publish novels and comics that you can read!

You can find more information on our website,
www.TCStudiosHQ.com.

#25 – Cooking/Baking.  (H) (F) | (W) (CP) (P)

---

*Brainstorm (Writing) ...*

- What's being made?
    - What are the ingredients that make up the recipe?
- What tools are being used to make it?
- What kind of taste does/will it have?

---

*Brainstorm (Drawing) ...*

- Experiment: Comic Strip.
    - Try drawing this as a short comic strip.

---

**Do you want to give us a prompt for next year's edition?**

You can submit prompt ideas you have based on next year's chapter themes. Credit will be given if selected.

You can find more information on our website, www.TCStudiosHQ.com.

#26 – Writing. (D) (AA) | (M) (I) (G)

---

*Brainstorm (Writing) ...*

- What are they using to write?
    - Laptop?
    - Pen and paper?
    - Tablet?
- Where are they writing?
    - At their desk?
    - A café?
    - In their bed?

---

*Brainstorm (Drawing) ...*

- Challenge: Life Reference.
    - See if you can take your own reference photos to use in your drawing.

---

**Drawing Exercise #3**

Draw a collection of supplies used for your hobby.

---

#27 – Singing. (F) (R) | (AP) (P) (C)

---

*Brainstorm (Writing)* ...

- What are they singing?
- Where are they singing?
  - Church? A Concert? Chorus class?
- Are they skilled or a beginner?
  - What range do they have?

---

*Brainstorm (Drawing)* ...

- Challenge: No references.
  - Put your muscle memory to the test and draw this scene without using any references.
    - Good luck!

---

**Did you know?**

We post daily writing & drawing prompts on our Social Medias for everyone to participate in.

Find us @PromptParty and use #PromptParty.

You can find more information on our website, www.TCStudiosHQ.com.

#28 – Fishing. (AA) (M) | (W) (G) (M)

---

*Brainstorm (Writing)* ...

- Where are they fishing?
    - Are they on a boat? Are they on land?
- What are they trying to catch?
- What are they using for bait?
- Are they experienced, or a novice?

---

*Brainstorm (Drawing)* ...

- Experiment: Colored Lighting.
    - When/if you are applying lighting effects to this piece, try using a different color instead of just a lighter gradient of the lit area.

---

**Did you know?**

In addition to posting daily on Social Media, we have daily interactive posts on our YouTube channel, Podcast, and Blog.

You can find more information on our website, www.TCStudiosHQ.com.

#29 – Traveling. (SF) (D) | (I) (P) (CP)

---

*Brainstorm (Writing) ...*

- Where are they going?
- Where have they been?
- How did they get there?
- Who do they go with?
- What will they do there?
- Why are they going?

---

*Brainstorm (Drawing) ...*

- Focus on: Emotion.
    - Is this person happy to be traveling?
    - Are they nervous to go if they're by themselves?
    - Do they want to be home instead?

---

**Remember!**

The listed genres/mediums and brainstorming boxes are **only suggestions!** We encourage you to do/use whatever you want.

35

#30 – Vlogging. (H) (SL) | (AP) (M) (C)

---

*Brainstorm (Writing)* ...

- Why are they vlogging?
- What are they vlogging?
- What tasks go into vlogging?
    - How do they feel about the related responsibilities?
    - How do they feel about showing their life?
    - How do they feel about people's responses to it?

---

*Brainstorm (Drawing)* ...

- Challenge: Primary Colors.
    - Try drawing this scene using only primary colors and their gradients.

---

**Be The First To Know.**

Join our newsletter and be the first to know about new prompt books, novels, comics, giveaways, freebies, coupons, and anything else we've got going on!

Find our newsletter on our website, www.TCStudiosHQ.com.

# Chapter Four: Race & Ethnicity.

#31 – Native American. (AA) (F) (SL) | (CP) (M) (W)

---

*Brainstorm (Writing) ...*

- Describe their features.
- Do they have an accent?
- What are their mannerisms like?
- Is culture a big part of their life?
- Are they involved in their heritage or is it just a part of their ancestry?

---

*Brainstorm (Drawing) ...*

- Practice: Texture.
    o Study texture techniques and implement them in your drawing.

---

**Writing Exercise #4**

Conduct an interview with someone of a different race and/or ethnicity.

#32 – Jewish. (SF) (D) (M) | (AP) (I) (P)

---

*Brainstorm (Writing) ...*

- Describe their features.
- Do they have an accent?
- What are their mannerisms like?
- Is culture a big part of their life?
- Are they involved in their heritage or is it just a part of their ancestry?

---

*Brainstorm (Drawing) ...*

- Practice different types of shading techniques.
  - Hatching.
  - Cross-Hatching.
  - Stippling.
  - Scribbling.
  - Contour Lines.

---

**You can share your work with us on Facebook, Instagram & Twitter!**

Tag us @PromptParty and use #PromptParty.

We'd love to see what you come up with!

#33 – British. (H) (R) (SL) | (C) (CP) (G)

---

*Brainstorm (Writing)* ...

- Describe their features.
- Do they have an accent?
- What are their mannerisms like?
- Is culture a big part of their life?
- Are they involved in their heritage or is it just a part of their ancestry?

---

*Brainstorm (Drawing)* ...

- Challenge: Opposite Colors.
  - Pick a color and it's opposite (ex: red and green).
  - Try coloring this piece with only those two colors and their gradients.

---

### Do you want your work published?

You can submit any work made using our prompts to our annual anthologies! Published submissions receive shared 25% royalties.

You can find more information on our website, www.TCStudiosHQ.com.

#34 – Irish. (AA) (D) (SL) | (M) (P) (AP)

---

*Brainstorm (Writing)* ...

- Describe their features.
- Do they have an accent?
- What are their mannerisms like?
- Is culture a big part of their life?
- Are they involved in their heritage or is it just a part of their ancestry?

---

*Brainstorm (Drawing)* ...

- Challenge: No Linework.
    - Try drawing this scene with no outlining – just dive right in with blocks of color!

---

**Did you know?**

A percentage of every anthology sold goes towards helping communities like yours. This includes donations to charities, funding of scholarships, creating of programs, and more!

You can find more information on our website, www.TCStudiosHQ.com.

#35 – French. (F) (SF) (M) | (G) (CP) (W)

---

*Brainstorm (Writing)* ...

- Describe their features.
- Do they have an accent?
- What are their mannerisms like?
- Is culture a big part of their life?
- Are they involved in their heritage or is it just a part of their ancestry?

---

*Brainstorm (Drawing)* ...

- Practice: Hair.
    - Study the flow and lighting dimensions of hair and implement the techniques into your drawing.

---

**Did you know?**

In addition to our annual prompt anthologies, every year we have themed anthologies that you can also submit to!

You can find more information on our website, www.TCStudiosHQ.com.

#36 – African. (AA) (F) (M) | (I) (AP) (M)

*Brainstorm (Writing) ...*

- Describe their features.
- Do they have an accent?
- What are their mannerisms like?
- Is culture a big part of their life?
- Are they involved in their heritage or is it just a part of their ancestry?

*Brainstorm (Drawing) ...*

- Challenge: Bird's Eye View.
    o Try drawing this piece with a bird's eye view.

**Drawing Exercise #4**

Draw a collection of things associated with a culture.

42

#37 – Australian. (R) (M) (H) | (P) (G) (C)

---

### *Brainstorm (Writing) ...*

- Describe their features.
- Do they have an accent?
- What are their mannerisms like?
- Is culture a big part of their life?
- Are they involved in their heritage or is it just a part of their ancestry?

---

### *Brainstorm (Drawing) ...*

- Practice: Anatomy.
  - Study proportions, positioning, and structure techniques and implement them in your drawing.

---

### Looking for a challenge?

Try doing one of our prompts with your friend(s)! See if you can come up with something together.

#38 – Italian. (D) (SL) (SF) | (W) (P) (CP)

---

*Brainstorm (Writing) ...*

- Describe their features.
- Do they have an accent?
- What are their mannerisms like?
- Is culture a big part of their life?
- Are they involved in their heritage or is it just a part of their ancestry?

---

*Brainstorm (Drawing) ...*

- Challenge: Monochrome.
    - Try drawing this scene using only one gradient of color.

---

**Did you know?**

We also make books to help with storytelling. With help on things like creating characters, world-building, magic systems, and more!

You can find more information on our website, www.TCStudiosHQ.com.

#39 – Hispanic. (R) (AA) (M) | (AP) (M) (C)

---

*Brainstorm (Writing)* ...

- Describe their features.
- Do they have an accent?
- What are their mannerisms like?
- Is culture a big part of their life?
- Are they involved in their heritage or is it just a part of their ancestry?

---

*Brainstorm (Drawing)* ...

- Challenge: Secondary Colors.
  - Try drawing this scene using only secondary colors and their gradients.

**Did you know?**

We also publish novels and comics that you can read!

You can find more information on our website, www.TCStudiosHQ.com.

#40 – Asian. (M) (F) (D) | (I) (G) (CP)

---

*Brainstorm (Writing) ...*

- Describe their features.
- Do they have an accent?
- What are their mannerisms like?
- Is culture a big part of their life?
- Are they involved in their heritage or is it just a part of their ancestry?

---

*Brainstorm (Drawing) ...*

- Focus on: Background.
  - Tell the story with the use of the background and its environment. Think about the use and placement of specific items to help get the point across.

---

**Do you want to give us a prompt for next year's edition?**

You can submit prompt ideas you have based on next year's chapter themes. Credit will be given if selected.

You can find more information on our website, www.TCStudiosHQ.com.

# Chapter Five: Modifications.

#41 – Piercings. (H) (R) | (G) (P) (C)

---

*Brainstorm (Writing) ...*

- Where are their piercings?
- How can you describe the jewelry used?
    - Think about the lighting.
    - Think about the shape and kind of metal.

---

*Brainstorm (Drawing) ...*

- Life Study.
    - Go out and find a person with this prompt to sketch.
    - See if someone you know will let you draw them!

---

**Writing Exercise #5**

Write about someone's experience getting something modified.

#42 – Amputation. (F) (D) | (W) (AP) (I)

---

*Brainstorm (Writing) ...*

- What was amputated?
    - Why?
    - When?
    - How?
- How does this affect their life?
    - Did amputation save them?
    - Was it an accident? War/battle injury?

---

*Brainstorm (Drawing) ...*

- Focus on: Storyline.
    - Can you tell the story of how/why this happened using only images?

---

**Did you know?**

We post daily writing & drawing prompts on our Social Medias for everyone to participate in.

Find us @PromptParty and use #PromptParty.

You can find more information on our website, www.TCStudiosHQ.com.

#43 – Tattoos. (SF) (AA) | (M) (CP) (P)

---

*Brainstorm (Writing)* ...

- Is there a story behind any of their tattoos?
  - Do they share any with friends/family?
- Where are they located?
  - Are they easy to see?
  - Are they able to be easily hidden?

---

*Brainstorm (Drawing)* ...

- Challenge: Life Reference.
  - See if you can take your own reference photos to use in your drawing.

---

**Did you know?**

In addition to posting daily on Social Media, we have daily interactive posts on our YouTube channel, Podcast, and Blog.

You can find more information on our website, www.TCStudiosHQ.com.

#44 – Botox. (SL) (M) | (C) (I) (G)

---

*Brainstorm (Writing) ...*

- Where is the Botox?
    - Is there too much?
    - Is it natural-looking?
- Why did they get Botox?
    - For vanity?
    - For migraines?

---

*Brainstorm (Drawing) ...*

- Experiment: Exaggerated Proportions/Features.
    - Get a little cartoony.
    - How might exaggerating certain features relate to the story behind the image?

---

**Remember!**

The listed genres/mediums and brainstorming boxes are **only suggestions!** We encourage you to do/use whatever you want.

#45 – Implants. (R) (F) | (P) (CP) (W)

---

*Brainstorm (Writing) ...*

- Are their implants noticeable?
    o How might it affect their everyday life?
- Why did they get them?
    o What kind did they get?

---

*Brainstorm (Drawing) ...*

- Focus on: Emotion.
    o Is this person happy with their implant(s)?
        ▪ Was it done out of vanity or necessity?

---

**Be The First To Know.**

Join our newsletter and be the first to know about new prompt books, novels, comics, giveaways, freebies, coupons, and anything else we've got going on!

Find our newsletter on our website, www.TCStudiosHQ.com.

#46 – Fantasy. (Pointed Ears, Fangs, etc.) (F) (SF) | (AP) (M) (G)

*Brainstorm (Writing)* ...

- Why did they get this modification?
    - Do they cosplay?
    - Do they roleplay?
    - Was it a dare?

*Brainstorm (Drawing)* ...

- Experiment: Colored Lighting.
    - When/if you are applying lighting effects to this piece, try using a different color instead of just a lighter gradient of the lit area.

**Drawing Exercise #5**

Draw a group of people with different body modifications.

#47 – Branding. (H) (D) | (C) (P) (I)

---

*Brainstorm (Writing) ...*

- What is this character being branded for?
- Was this their choice or was it forced upon them?
    - Are they part of a group or cult?
- What was the process like?
    - Casual? A ritual?

---

*Brainstorm (Drawing) ...*

- Challenge: Bird's Eye View.
    - Try drawing this piece with a bird's eye view.

---

**You can share your work with us on Facebook, Instagram & Twitter!**

Tag us @PromptParty and use #PromptParty.

We'd love to see what you come up with!

#48 – Scarification. (H) (AA) | (W) (M) (CP)

---

*Brainstorm (Writing) ...*

- What does the skin around the scarring look like?
    - What did they get scarred?
        - Does it represent anything?
- Is it fresh or old?
    - What is/was their healing process like?

---

*Brainstorm (Drawing) ...*

- Challenge: Monochrome.
    - Try drawing this scene using only one gradient of color.

---

**Do you want your work published?**

You can submit any work made using our prompts to our annual anthologies! Published submissions receive shared 25% royalties.

You can find more information on our website, www.TCStudiosHQ.com.

#49 – Robotic Limb. (SF) (F) | (AP) (I) (C)

---

*Brainstorm (Writing) ...*

- What does it look like?
    - Does it have any extra features/abilities?
- Where is it located?
    - What happened to that original limb?

---

*Brainstorm (Drawing) ...*

- Focus on: Realism.
    - Try making the metal for this limb look as realistic as you can.

---

**Did you know?**

A percentage of every anthology sold goes towards helping communities like yours. This includes donations to charities, funding of scholarships, creating of programs, and more!

You can find more information on our website, www.TCStudiosHQ.com.

#50 – Mechanical Implant. (SL) (M) | (G) (AP) (P)

---

*Brainstorm (Writing) ...*

- Describe how this implant works and/or how it was put in place.
- Why did this person get it?
  - Was it required for their health?

---

*Brainstorm (Drawing) ...*

- Challenge: Input.
  - Let someone tell you how you should set up your drawing and follow their instructions to the best of your ability.

---

**Did you know?**

In addition to our annual prompt anthologies, every year we have <u>themed</u> anthologies that you can also submit to!

You can find more information on our website, www.TCStudiosHQ.com.

56

# Chapter Six: Occupations.

#51 – Cashier. (SL) (F) (D) | (CP) (I) (M)

---

*Brainstorm (Writing)* ...

- What kind of store are they in?
    - Is there a uniform?
    - What kind of equipment are they using?
- What are they doing?
    - Helping a customer?
    - Restocking?
    - Plotting world domination?

---

*Brainstorm (Drawing)* ...

- Experiment: Comic Strip.
    - Try drawing this as a short comic strip.

---

**Writing Exercise #6**

Write about a character's preparation process for an interview.

---

#52 – Makeup Artist. (M) (H) (R) | (G) (P) (C)

---

*Brainstorm (Writing) ...*

- What kind of makeup are they applying?
  - Glamorous?
  - Special effects?
- Who are they working on?
  - A model?
  - An actor?

---

*Brainstorm (Drawing) ...*

- Challenge: Color Palette.
  - Use a random color palette generator or ask a friend to pick 3-5 colors for you to use.

---

**Looking for a challenge?**

Try doing one of our prompts with your friend(s)! See if you can come up with something together.

#53 – Author. (R) (D) (AA) | (W) (AP) (I)

---

*Brainstorm (Writing) ...*

- What genre(s) do they write?
  - Romance?
  - Fantasy?
  - Horror?
- What does their workspace look like?
  - Neat and tidy?
  - Absolute chaos?

---

*Brainstorm (Drawing) ...*

- Practice: Anatomy.
  - Study proportions, positioning, and structure techniques and implement them in your drawing.

---

**Did you know?**

We also make books to help with storytelling. With help on things like creating characters, world-building, magic systems, and more!

You can find more information on our website, www.TCStudiosHQ.com.

#54 – EMT. (AA) (SL) (M) | (M) (P) (CP)

---

*Brainstorm (Writing) ...*

- What are they doing?
    - o Driving an ambulance?
    - o Talking with a patient?
    - o Treating a patient?
- How might they be feeling about their job?
    - o Are they happy?
    - o Are they anxious?

---

*Brainstorm (Drawing) ...*

- Challenge: Self-Portrait.
    - o Draw yourself into this scene.

---

**Did you know?**

We also publish novels and comics that you can read!

You can find more information on our website,
www.TCStudiosHQ.com.

#55 – Fashion Designer. (R) (SF) (SL) | (G) (W) (AP)

---

*Brainstorm (Writing) ...*

- What kind of clothing do they design?
  - Sports?
  - Formal?
  - Casual?
- Are they well-known?
- What goes on in their day to day life?

---

*Brainstorm (Drawing) ...*

- Practice: Lighting.
  - Study color choice, gradients, and placement techniques of lighting and implement them in your drawing.

---

**Do you want to give us a prompt for next year's edition?**

You can submit prompt ideas you have based on next year's chapter themes. Credit will be given if selected.

You can find more information on our website, www.TCStudiosHQ.com.

#56 – Film Maker. (M) (H) (AA) | (C) (I) (P)

---

*Brainstorm (Writing)* ...

- What kind of films do they make?
  - Fiction?
  - Documentaries?
- What kind of process do they have?
- How do they work with their staff?

---

*Brainstorm (Drawing)* ...

- Practice: Hands.
  - Study up on some hand techniques and implement them in your drawing.
    - Maybe they are holding a camera or directing their crew.

---

**Drawing Exercise #6**

Draw 10 different types of work uniforms.

---

#57 – Chef. (D) (H) (R) | (M) (CP) (W)

*Brainstorm (Writing) ...*

- What are their specialties?
- Where do they work?
    - At a restaurant?
    - At a Deli?
    - Are they a personal chef?

*Brainstorm (Drawing) ...*

- Focus on: Background.
    - Tell the story with the use of the background and its environment. Think about the use and placement of specific items to help get the point across.

**Did you know?**

We post daily writing & drawing prompts on our Social Medias for everyone to participate in.

Find us @PromptParty and use #PromptParty.

You can find more information on our website, www.TCStudiosHQ.com.

#58 – Carpenter. (SF) (D) (SL) | (AP) (I) (G)

---

*Brainstorm (Writing)* ...

- Are they working on anything new?
- What does their work/studio space look like?
- What style is their work in?
- Do they sell their work?
- What does a day in their life look like when they're creating?

---

*Brainstorm (Drawing)* ...

- Practice different types of shading techniques.
  - Hatching.
  - Cross-Hatching.
  - Stippling.
  - Scribbling.
  - Contour Lines.

---

**Did you know?**

In addition to posting daily on Social Media, we have daily interactive posts on our YouTube channel, Podcast, and Blog.

You can find more information on our website, www.TCStudiosHQ.com.

#59 – Bartender. (R) (F) (M) | (P) (W) (C)

---

*Brainstorm (Writing)* ...

- Do they enjoy their job?
    - What are their responsibilities?
    - Do they have any regular customers?
        - What are they like?
        - Do they like some more than others?
    - What are some of their tasks?

---

*Brainstorm (Drawing)* ...

- Experiment: Comic Strip.
    - Try drawing this as a short comic strip.

---

**Remember!**

The listed genres/mediums and brainstorming boxes are **only suggestions!** We encourage you to do/use whatever you want.

#60 – Detective. (M) (H) (AA) | (CP) (G) (M)

*Brainstorm (Writing) ...*

- What are they investigating?
    - What are the clues that they've found?
    - Who are they suspecting?
    - What is the case that they're working?
- How does their job affect their personal life?
    - Do they take it home with them?
    - Do they go to therapy?
    - Do they talk to their partner about cases?

*Brainstorm (Drawing) ...*

- Challenge: No Linework.
    - Try drawing this scene with no outlining – just dive right in with blocks of color!

# Chapter Seven: Personalities.

#61 – The Counselor – INFJ. (AA) (R) | (P) (W) (AP)

---

*Brainstorm (Writing) ...*

- What is this character's personality like?
    - How does this relate to their actions?
        - Their speech?
        - Their body language?
        - Their mannerisms?
    - Can their personality be deciphered by their clothing choices?
        - By their facial expressions?
- What might this character do for a living?
    - Does it suit their personality type?
- What kind of personalities do they clash with?
    - What kind do they get along with?

---

*Brainstorm (Drawing) ...*

- Play around with your shading techniques.
    - How can you emphasize the tension or the comic relief of the scene using shading and lighting?

---

**Writing Exercise #7**

Write a character with a personality that you love.

---

#62 – The Visionary – ENTP. (H) (SF) | (I) (C) (M)

---

*Brainstorm (Writing)* ...

- What is this character's personality like?
  - How does this relate to their actions?
    - Their speech?
    - Their body language?
    - Their mannerisms?
  - Can their personality be deciphered by their clothing choices?
    - By their facial expressions?
- What might this character do for a living?
  - Does it suit their personality type?
- What kind of personalities do they clash with?
  - What kind do they get along with?

---

*Brainstorm (Drawing)* ...

- Challenge: No references.
  - Put your muscle memory to the test and draw this scene without using any references.
    - Good luck!

---

**You can share your work with us on Facebook, Instagram & Twitter!**

Tag us @PromptParty and use #PromptParty.

We'd love to see what you come up with!

#63 – The Commander – ENTJ. (F) (M) | (CP) (G) (W)

---

*Brainstorm (Writing)* ...

- What is this character's personality like?
    - How does this relate to their actions?
        - Their speech?
        - Their body language?
        - Their mannerisms?
    - Can their personality be deciphered by their clothing choices?
        - By their facial expressions?
- What might this character do for a living?
    - Does it suit their personality type?
- What kind of personalities do they clash with?
    - What kind do they get along with?

---

*Brainstorm (Drawing)* ...

- Experiment: Colored Lighting.
    - When/if you are applying lighting effects to this piece, try using a different color instead of just a lighter gradient of the lit area.

---

**Do you want your work published?**

You can submit any work made using our prompts to our annual anthologies! Published submissions receive shared 25% royalties.

You can find more information on our website, www.TCStudiosHQ.com.

#64 – The Nurturer – ISFJ. (D) (SL) | (AP) (C) (P)

---

*Brainstorm (Writing)* ...

- What is this character's personality like?
    - How does this relate to their actions?
        - Their speech?
        - Their body language?
        - Their mannerisms?
    - Can their personality be deciphered by their clothing choices?
        - By their facial expressions?
- What might this character do for a living?
    - Does it suit their personality type?
- What kind of personalities do they clash with?
    - What kind do they get along with?

---

*Brainstorm (Drawing)* ...

- Practice: Hair.
    - Study the flow and lighting dimensions of hair and implement the techniques into your drawing.

---

**Did you know?**

A percentage of every anthology sold goes towards helping communities like yours. This includes donations to charities, funding of scholarships, creating of programs, and more!

You can find more information on our website,
www.TCStudiosHQ.com.

#65 – The Thinker – INTP. (SF) (M) | (M) (G) (I)

---

*Brainstorm (Writing)* ...

- What is this character's personality like?
    - How does this relate to their actions?
        - Their speech?
        - Their body language?
        - Their mannerisms?
    - Can their personality be deciphered by their clothing choices?
        - By their facial expressions?
- What might this character do for a living?
    - Does it suit their personality type?
- What kind of personalities do they clash with?
    - What kind do they get along with?

---

*Brainstorm (Drawing)* ...

- Practice different types of shading techniques.
    - Hatching.
    - Cross-Hatching.
    - Stippling.
    - Scribbling.
    - Contour Lines.

---

**Did you know?**

In addition to our annual prompt anthologies, every year we have <u>themed</u> anthologies that you can also submit to!

You can find more information on our website, www.TCStudiosHQ.com.

#66 – The Doer – ESTP. (AA) (F) | (CP) (P) (W)

---

*Brainstorm (Writing) ...*

- What is this character's personality like?
  - How does this relate to their actions?
    - Their speech?
    - Their body language?
    - Their mannerisms?
  - Can their personality be deciphered by their clothing choices?
    - By their facial expressions?
- What might this character do for a living?
  - Does it suit their personality type?
- What kind of personalities do they clash with?
  - What kind do they get along with?

---

*Brainstorm (Drawing) ...*

- Experiment: Bold Line Work.
  - When you've finished lining your work (if you're lining), try making some areas thicker than others.
    - It can be dramatically, or just a bit.
      - Take note of how it changes the tone of your work.

---

**Drawing Exercise #7**

Draw the same character 10 times – each with a different personality.

---

72

#67 – The Performer – ESFP. (R) (H) | (C) (M) (AP)

---

*Brainstorm (Writing) ...*

- What is this character's personality like?
  - How does this relate to their actions?
    - Their speech?
    - Their body language?
    - Their mannerisms?
  - Can their personality be deciphered by their clothing choices?
    - By their facial expressions?
- What might this character do for a living?
  - Does it suit their personality type?
- What kind of personalities do they clash with?
  - What kind do they get along with?

---

*Brainstorm (Drawing) ...*

- Challenge: Secondary Colors.
  - Try drawing this scene using only secondary colors and their gradients.

---

### Looking for a challenge?

Try doing one of our prompts with your friend(s)! See if you can come up with something together.

#68 – The Idealist – INFP. (D) (SL) | (I) (G) (CP)

---

*Brainstorm (Writing) ...*

- What is this character's personality like?
  - How does this relate to their actions?
    - Their speech?
    - Their body language?
    - Their mannerisms?
  - Can their personality be deciphered by their clothing choices?
    - By their facial expressions?
- What might this character do for a living?
  - Does it suit their personality type?
- What kind of personalities do they clash with?
  - What kind do they get along with?

---

*Brainstorm (Drawing) ...*

- Practice: Texture.
  - Study texture techniques and implement them in your drawing.

---

**Did you know?**

We also make books to help with storytelling. With help on things like creating characters, world-building, magic systems, and more!

You can find more information on our website, www.TCStudiosHQ.com.

#69 – The Provider – ESFJ. (F) (AA) | (W) (M) (C)

---

*Brainstorm (Writing) ...*

- What is this character's personality like?
  - How does this relate to their actions?
    - Their speech?
    - Their body language?
    - Their mannerisms?
  - Can their personality be deciphered by their clothing choices?
    - By their facial expressions?
- What might this character do for a living?
  - Does it suit their personality type?
- What kind of personalities do they clash with?
  - What kind do they get along with?

---

*Brainstorm (Drawing) ...*

- Challenge: Color Palette.
  - Use a random color palette generator or ask a friend to pick 3-5 colors for you to use.

---

**Did you know?**

We also publish novels and comics that you can read!

You can find more information on our website, www.TCStudiosHQ.com.

#70 – The Champion – ENFP. (SF) (M) | (P) (G) (AP)

---

*Brainstorm (Writing) ...*

- What is this character's personality like?
    - How does this relate to their actions?
        - Their speech?
        - Their body language?
        - Their mannerisms?
    - Can their personality be deciphered by their clothing choices?
        - By their facial expressions?
- What might this character do for a living?
    - Does it suit their personality type?
- What kind of personalities do they clash with?
    - What kind do they get along with?

---

*Brainstorm (Drawing) ...*

- Practice: Anatomy.
    - Study proportions, positioning, and structure techniques and implement them in your drawing.

---

**Do you want to give us a prompt for next year's edition?**

You can submit prompt ideas you have based on next year's chapter themes. Credit will be given if selected.

You can find more information on our website, www.TCStudiosHQ.com.

# Chapter Eight: Negative Traits.

#71 – Possessive. (H) (SF) (M) | (P) (M) (G)

---

*Brainstorm (Writing) ...*

- What are they possessive about?
  - People?
  - Items?
  - Things in general?
- How do people deal with their trait?
  - Do they hide things from them?
  - Do they confront them about it?
- Do they know they're possessive?

---

*Brainstorm (Drawing) ...*

- Practice: Texture.
  - Study texture techniques and implement them in your drawing.

---

**Writing Exercise #8**

Write a character with three traits that you hate.

---

#72 – Insecure. (R) (F) (SL) | (AP) (I) (W)

---

*Brainstorm (Writing) ...*

- How does being insecure limit their actions?
    - What are they insecure about?
        - How do they act when confronting that subject?
        - How does it change their facial and body language?

---

*Brainstorm (Drawing) ...*

- Focus on: Expression.
    - How can you use this person's facial and body language to emphasize the prompt?

---

**Did you know?**

We post daily writing & drawing prompts on our Social Medias for everyone to participate in.

Find us @PromptParty and use #PromptParty.

You can find more information on our website, www.TCStudiosHQ.com.

#73 – Forgetful. (D) (M) (AA) | (CP) (C) (G)

---

*Brainstorm (Writing) ...*

- Do they have any tactics to try and remember things?
    - What might be some things they do?
    - Do they worry about forgetting things?
- How do people feel about this trait?
    - Do they try to help them remember?
    - Do they get upset?

---

*Brainstorm (Drawing) ...*

- Challenge: Input.
    - Let someone tell you how you should set up your drawing and follow their instructions to the best of your ability.

---

**Did you know?**

In addition to posting daily on Social Media, we have daily interactive posts on our YouTube channel, Podcast, and Blog.

You can find more information on our website, www.TCStudiosHQ.com.

#74 – Accusatory. (R) (D) (M) | (P) (I) (W)

---

*Brainstorm (Writing) ...*

- Why does this character feel the need to jump to conclusions?
    - How often are they right or wrong?
        - What happens when they're right?
        - What happens when they're wrong?
    - How do they act when they're accusing someone?
        - Is it aggressive?
        - Is it cautious?

---

*Brainstorm (Drawing) ...*

- Focus on: Body Language.
    - How can you position the body to emphasize and highlight this character's tendency to accuse others?
    - Maybe draw them in the act of accusing.

---

### Remember!

The listed genres/mediums and brainstorming boxes are **only suggestions!** We encourage you to do/use whatever you want.

#75 – Obsessive. (F) (SF) (H) | (M) (CP) (AP)

---

*Brainstorm (Writing)* ...

- How does this person act when they're being obsessive over something?
    - How do they act when things aren't going the way they planned?

---

*Brainstorm (Drawing)* ...

- Challenge: Bird's Eye View.
    - Try drawing this piece with a bird's eye view.

---

**Be The First To Know.**

Join our newsletter and be the first to know about new prompt books, novels, comics, giveaways, freebies, coupons, and anything else we've got going on!

Find our newsletter on our website, www.TCStudiosHQ.com.

#76 – Selfish. (AA) (SL) (D) | (C) (G) (W)

> ### *Brainstorm (Writing) ...*
>
> - What tendencies does this character have?
>     - What is their thought process like?
>     - What are their mannerisms like?
> - How do they act when attention is taken from them?
>     - Are they aggressive?
>     - Are they moody?

> ### *Brainstorm (Drawing) ...*
>
> - Practice: Lighting.
>     - Study color choice, gradients, and placement techniques of lighting and implement them in your drawing.

---

### Drawing Exercise #8

Draw an object that relates to one of the traits listed in this chapter.

Ex: Forgetful – Scattered sticky notes.

---

#77 – Evil. (H) (AA) (F) | (CP) (I) (M)

---

*Brainstorm (Writing)* ...

- What types of things does this character do that would make them evil?
    - What level of evil are we talking about here?
        - Leaving an empty milk carton in the fridge or world domination?

---

*Brainstorm (Drawing)* ...

- Experiment: Colored Lighting.
    - When/if you are applying lighting effects to this piece, try using a different color instead of just a lighter gradient of the lit area.

---

**Do you want to give us a prompt for next year's edition?**

You can submit prompt ideas you have based on next year's chapter themes. Credit will be given if selected.

You can find more information on our website, www.TCStudiosHQ.com.

#78 – Controlling. (M) (F) (R) | (I) (P) (AP)

---

*Brainstorm (Writing)* ...

- What kind of actions does this character take to gain or maintain control?
- Do they know they are controlling?
  - Is it done compulsively?

---

*Brainstorm (Drawing)* ...

- Play around with your shading techniques.
  - How can you emphasize the tension or the comic relief of the scene using shading and lighting?

---

**You can share your work with us on Facebook, Instagram & Twitter!**

Tag us @PromptParty and use #PromptParty.

We'd love to see what you come up with!

#79 – Self-conscious. (SF) (AA) (D) | (M) (CP) (C)

---

*Brainstorm (Writing)* ...

- What are they self-conscious about?
    - How does it affect their actions?
    - What are their mannerisms like?
- How does this hinder them?
- Are they working towards being less self-conscious?

---

*Brainstorm (Drawing)* ...

- Focus on: Emotion.
    - Focus on trying to capture the emotion of unease in this character's facial expression.

---

**Do you want your work published?**

You can submit any work made using our prompts to our annual anthologies! Published submissions receive shared 25% royalties.

You can find more information on our website, www.TCStudiosHQ.com.

#80 – Mean-spirited. (H) (SL) (M) | (G) (I) (W)

---

*Brainstorm (Writing) ...*

- What does this character do that makes them mean?
    - Why do they act this way?
        - Does it stem from something else?
        - Are they just mean for the sake of being mean?
    - How do people act around them?
        - Do they avoid them?
        - Are they confrontational?

---

*Brainstorm (Drawing) ...*

- Experiment: Colored Lighting.
    - When/if you are applying lighting effects to this piece, try using a different color instead of just a lighter gradient of the lit area.

---

**Did you know?**

A percentage of every anthology sold goes towards helping communities like yours. This includes donations to charities, funding of scholarships, creating of programs, and more!

You can find more information on our website, www.TCStudiosHQ.com.

# Chapter Nine: Aesthetics.

#81 – Goth. (R) (H) (F) | (G) (AP) (P)

---

*Brainstorm (Writing) ...*

- How does this character dress?
  - Is their aesthetic obvious or subtle?
- What kind of personality do they have?
- Do they have stereotypical likes/dislikes?
  - Music?
  - Hobbies?
  - Tastes?
- How did they come across this aesthetic?
- Is it accepted by their friends/family?

---

*Brainstorm (Drawing) ...*

- Focus on: Environment.
  - Explore the prompt with the background or the characters' environment in addition to the character.

---

**Writing Exercise #9**

Write about a day in the life of a character with an aesthetic that you idolize.

---

#82 – Hipster. (M) (D) (SL) | (CP) (W) (I)

---

*Brainstorm (Writing)* ...

- How does this character dress?
  - ○ Is their aesthetic obvious or subtle?
- What kind of personality do they have?
- Do they have stereotypical likes/dislikes?
  - ○ Music?
  - ○ Hobbies?
  - ○ Tastes?
- How did they come across this aesthetic?
- Is it accepted by their friends/family?

---

*Brainstorm (Drawing)* ...

- Focus on: Background.
  - ○ Tell the story with the use of the background and its environment. Think about the use and placement of specific items to help get the point across.

---

**Did you know?**

In addition to our annual prompt anthologies, every year we have <u>themed</u> anthologies that you can also submit to!

You can find more information on our website, www.TCStudiosHQ.com.

#83 – Earthy. (SF) (AA) (F) | (M) (C) (AP)

---

*Brainstorm (Writing)* ...

- How does this character dress?
  - o Is their aesthetic obvious or subtle?
- What kind of personality do they have?
- Do they have stereotypical likes/dislikes?
  - o Music?
  - o Hobbies?
  - o Tastes?
- How did they come across this aesthetic?
- Is it accepted by their friends/family?

---

*Brainstorm (Drawing)* ...

- Challenge: Secondary Colors.
  - o Try drawing this scene using only secondary colors and their gradients.

---

### Looking for a challenge?

Try doing one of our prompts with your friend(s)! See if you can come up with something together.

#84 – Witchy. (F) (M) (R) | (G) (W) (P)

---

*Brainstorm (Writing)* ...

- How does this character dress?
    - Is their aesthetic obvious or subtle?
- What kind of personality do they have?
- Do they have stereotypical likes/dislikes?
    - Music?
    - Hobbies?
    - Tastes?
- How did they come across this aesthetic?
- Is it accepted by their friends/family?

---

*Brainstorm (Drawing)* ...

- Experiment: Comic Strip.
    - Try drawing this as a short comic strip.

---

**Did you know?**

We also make books to help with storytelling. With help on things like creating characters, world-building, magic systems, and more!

You can find more information on our website, www.TCStudiosHQ.com.

#85 – Vintage. (SL) (D) (H) | (I) (M) (CP)

---

*Brainstorm (Writing) ...*

- How does this character dress?
  - Is their aesthetic obvious or subtle?
- What kind of personality do they have?
- Do they have stereotypical likes/dislikes?
  - Music?
  - Hobbies?
  - Tastes?
- How did they come across this aesthetic?
- Is it accepted by their friends/family?

---

*Brainstorm (Drawing) ...*

- Practice: Lighting.
  - Study color choice, gradients, and placement techniques of lighting and implement them in your drawing.

---

**Did you know?**

We also publish novels and comics that you can read!

You can find more information on our website, www.TCStudiosHQ.com.

#86 – Grunge. (SF) (AA) (M) | (AP) (C) (G)

---

### *Brainstorm (Writing) ...*

- How does this character dress?
  - Is their aesthetic obvious or subtle?
- What kind of personality do they have?
- Do they have stereotypical likes/dislikes?
  - Music?
  - Hobbies?
  - Tastes?
- How did they come across this aesthetic?
- Is it accepted by their friends/family?

---

### *Brainstorm (Drawing) ...*

- Practice different types of shading techniques.
  - Hatching.
  - Cross-Hatching.
  - Stippling.
  - Scribbling.
  - Contour Lines.

---

**Drawing Exercise #9**

Draw a collection of items that relate to one of the listed aesthetics.

---

92

#87 – Eclectic.  (F) (R) (D) | (W) (CP) (P)

---

*Brainstorm (Writing) ...*

- How does this character dress?
    - o   Is their aesthetic obvious or subtle?
- What kind of personality do they have?
- Do they have stereotypical likes/dislikes?
    - o   Music?
    - o   Hobbies?
    - o   Tastes?
- How did they come across this aesthetic?
- Is it accepted by their friends/family?

---

*Brainstorm (Drawing) ...*

- Challenge: No references.
    - o   Put your muscle memory to the test and draw this scene without using any references.
        - ▪   Good luck!

---

**Do you want to give us a prompt for next year's edition?**

You can submit prompt ideas you have based on next year's chapter themes. Credit will be given if selected.

You can find more information on our website, www.TCStudiosHQ.com.

#88 – Retro. (H) (SL) (M) | (I) (AP) (M)

---

*Brainstorm (Writing)* ...

- How does this character dress?
  - Is their aesthetic obvious or subtle?
- What kind of personality do they have?
- Do they have stereotypical likes/dislikes?
  - Music?
  - Hobbies?
  - Tastes?
- How did they come across this aesthetic?
- Is it accepted by their friends/family?

---

*Brainstorm (Drawing)* ...

- Practice: Hair.
  - Study the flow and lighting dimensions of hair and implement the techniques into your drawing.

---

**Did you know?**

We post daily writing & drawing prompts on our Social Medias for everyone to participate in.

Find us @PromptParty and use #PromptParty.

You can find more information on our website, www.TCStudiosHQ.com.

#89 – Nerdy. (AA) (F) (SF) | (G) (C) (P)

---

*Brainstorm (Writing) ...*

- How does this character dress?
  - Is their aesthetic obvious or subtle?
- What kind of personality do they have?
- Do they have stereotypical likes/dislikes?
  - Music?
  - Hobbies?
  - Tastes?
- How did they come across this aesthetic?
- Is it accepted by their friends/family?

---

*Brainstorm (Drawing) ...*

- Practice: Hands.
  - Study up on some hand techniques and implement them in your drawing.
    - Maybe they're holding a game controller or playing a card game.

---

**Did you know?**

In addition to posting daily on Social Media, we have daily interactive posts on our YouTube channel, Podcast, and Blog.

You can find more information on our website, www.TCStudiosHQ.com.

#90 – Elegant. (D) (R) (H) | (CP) (W) (I)

---

*Brainstorm (Writing)* ...

- How does this character dress?
    - Is their aesthetic obvious or subtle?
- What kind of personality do they have?
- Do they have stereotypical likes/dislikes?
    - Music?
    - Hobbies?
    - Tastes?
- How did they come across this aesthetic?
- Is it accepted by their friends/family?

---

*Brainstorm (Drawing)* ...

- Challenge: Color Palette.
    - Use a random color palette generator or ask a friend to pick 3-5 colors for you to use.

---

**Remember!**

The listed genres/mediums and brainstorming boxes are **only suggestions!** We encourage you to do/use whatever you want.

# Chapter Ten: Features.

#91 – Freckles. (R) (AA) | (P) (W) (C)

---

*Brainstorm (Writing)* ...

- Where are the freckles?
- Are they genetic?
    o Are they from too much sun exposure?
- How dark are they compared to this character's skin tone?

---

*Brainstorm (Drawing)* ...

- Practice: Skin Tones.
    o Study skin tone palettes and techniques and implement them in your drawing.

---

**Writing Exercise #10**

Write about a detective who is looking for someone with specific features.

---

#92 – Wrinkles. (SL) (M) | (G) (AP) (I)

---

*Brainstorm (Writing)* ...

- How old is this character?
    o Are they too young for wrinkles?
- Where are the wrinkles?
    o How do they affect the layout of their face/body?
- How do they feel about them?
    o Are they trying to get rid of them?
    o Have they accepted them?

---

*Brainstorm (Drawing)* ...

- Life Study.
    o Go out and find a person with this prompt to sketch.
    o See if someone you know will let you draw them!

---

**Be The First To Know.**

Join our newsletter and be the first to know about new prompt books, novels, comics, giveaways, freebies, coupons, and anything else we've got going on!

Find our newsletter on our website, www.TCStudiosHQ.com.

#93 – Tan Lines. (D) (F) | (CP) (M) (G)

---

*Brainstorm (Writing)* ...

- Where are they?
- How drastic of a change from their natural skin tone is there?
- What might their tan lines say about their frequent activities?
    - Do they spend a lot of time on the beach?
    - Do they play an outdoor sport?
    - Do they work outside?

---

*Brainstorm (Drawing)* ...

- Challenge: Self-Portrait.
    - Draw yourself into this scene.

---

**You can share your work with us on Facebook, Instagram & Twitter!**

Tag us @PromptParty and use #PromptParty.

We'd love to see what you come up with!

#94 – Hair Type (Frizzy, Curly, etc.). (SF) (AA) | (P) (I) (CP)

---

*Brainstorm (Writing)* ...

- How does this character care for their hair?
    - How do they style it?
- What color is it?
    - Are parts of it dyed?
- Do they want to do anything different with it?
    - Perm it?
    - Dreadlock it?
    - Straighten it?

---

*Brainstorm (Drawing)* ...

- Challenge: No Linework.
    - Try drawing this scene with no outlining – just dive right in with blocks of color!

---

**Do you want your work published?**

You can submit any work made using our prompts to our annual anthologies! Published submissions receive shared 25% royalties.

You can find more information on our website, www.TCStudiosHQ.com.

#95 – Stretch Marks. (R) (F) | (C) (AP) (G)

---

*Brainstorm (Writing)* ...

- How did this character get these stretch marks?
    - Losing weight?
    - Gaining weight?
    - Pregnancy?
- How do they feel about them?
- Where are they located?
- Describe them.

---

*Brainstorm (Drawing)* ...

- Challenge: Life Reference.
    - See if you can take your own reference photos to use in your drawing.

---

**Did you know?**

A percentage of every anthology sold goes towards helping communities like yours. This includes donations to charities, funding of scholarships, creating of programs, and more!

You can find more information on our website, www.TCStudiosHQ.com.

#96 – Scars. (D) (H) | (W) (I) (M)

---

*Brainstorm (Writing)* ...

- Where are the scars located?
    - Are they visible?
    - Are they easy to hide?
- How did they get them?
    - Accident?
    - Self-harm?
    - Surgery?
- How do they feel about them?
    - Proud?
    - Shameful?
- Describe them.

---

*Brainstorm (Drawing)* ...

- Focus on: Body language.
    - Does having scars affect this person's confidence?
        - Are they self-conscious?
        - Are they proud?

---

**Drawing Exercise #10**

Draw a character with 5 features you admire.

---

102

#97 – Braces. (SL) (SF) | (P) (CP) (C)

---

*Brainstorm (Writing)* ...

- How old is this character?
- How does wearing braces affect their life?
- How far along are they in the process?
  - Have they just gotten them?
  - Are they close to taking them off?
- Do they make them self-conscious?
- Are they still confident?
- How do they affect their speech?

---

*Brainstorm (Drawing)* ...

- Practice: Anatomy.
  - Study proportions, positioning, and structure techniques and implement them in your drawing.

---

**Did you know?**

In addition to our annual prompt anthologies, every year we have themed anthologies that you can also submit to!

You can find more information on our website, www.TCStudiosHQ.com.

#98 – Glasses. (M) (AA) | (G) (AP) (M)

---

*Brainstorm (Writing) ...*

- What kind of glasses are they?
  - Square?
  - Round?
- What color are their eyes?
- How do they feel about wearing glasses?
  - Are they required?
  - Are they for fashion?
  - Are they self-conscious about them?

---

*Brainstorm (Drawing) ...*

- Challenge: Color Palette.
  - Use a random color palette generator or ask a friend to pick 3-5 colors for you to use.

**Looking for a challenge?**

Try doing one of our prompts with your friend(s)! See if you can come up with something together.

#99 – Painted Nails. (F) (SF) | (I) (W) (CP)

---

*Brainstorm (Writing) ...*

- What do their nails look like?
  - Short & square?
  - Long & pointed?
  - Broken & bitten?
- What color are they?
  - A solid color?
  - Is there a design?
  - Is there a French Tip?
- What might the state of their nails say about their life?
  - Is it hectic?
  - Is it well managed?
  - Are they stressed?

---

*Brainstorm (Drawing) ...*

- Practice: Skin Tones.
  - Study skin tone palettes and techniques and implement them in your drawing.

---

**Did you know?**

We also make books to help with storytelling. With help on things like creating characters, world-building, magic systems, and more!

You can find more information on our website,
www.TCStudiosHQ.com.

#100 – Hairy. (R) (H) | (P) (C) (AP)

---

### *Brainstorm (Writing) ...*

- Where is this character hairy?
- What kind of hair is it?
    - Curly? Frizzy? Straight?
    - What color is it?
- Do they try to manage it?
- Do they let it run wild?

---

### *Brainstorm (Drawing) ...*

- Experiment: Exaggerated Proportions/Features.
    - Get a little cartoony.
    - How might exaggerating certain features help the imagery?

---

**Did you know?**

We also publish novels and comics that you can read!

You can find more information on our website, www.TCStudiosHQ.com.

# Prompts by Genre

## Fantasy (F)

1. #1 – Curvy.
2. #6 – Well-toned.
3. #9 – Broad.
4. #11 – Naïve.
5. #14 – Magical.
6. #16 – Noisy.
7. #19 – Flirtatious.
8. #25 – Cooking/Baking.
9. #27 – Singing.
10. #31 – Native American.
11. #35 – French.
12. #36 – African.
13. #40 – Asian.
14. #42 – Amputation.
15. #45 – Implants.
16. #46 – Fantasy. (Pointed Ears, Fangs, etc.)
17. #49 – Robotic Limb.
18. #51 – Cashier.
19. #59 – Bartender.
20. #63 – The Commander – ENTJ.
21. #66 – The Doer – ESTP.
22. #69 – The Provider – ESFJ.
23. #72 – Insecure.
24. #75 – Obsessive.
25. #78 – Controlling.
26. #81 – Goth.
27. #83 – Earthy.
28. #84 – Witchy.
29. #87 – Eclectic.
30. #89 – Nerdy.
31. #93 – Tan Lines.
32. #95 – Stretch Marks.
33. #99 – Painted Nails.

# Science Fiction (SF)

1. #2 – Straight & Narrow.
2. #5 – Muscular.
3. #8 – Chunky.
4. #10 – Bulky.
5. #12 – Sneaky.
6. #16 – Noisy.
7. #20 – Shy.
8. #23 – Photography.
9. #29 – Traveling.
10. #32 – Jewish.
11. #35 – French.
12. #38 – Italian.
13. #43 – Tattoos.
14. #46 – Fantasy. (Pointed Ears, Fangs, etc.)
15. #49 – Robotic Limb.
16. #55 – Fashion Designer.
17. #58 – Carpenter.
18. #62 – The Visionary – ENTP.
19. #65 – The Thinker – INTP.
20. #70 – The Champion – ENFP.
21. #71 – Possessive.
22. #75 – Obsessive.
23. #79 – Self-conscious.
24. #83 – Earthy.
25. #86 – Grunge.
26. #89 – Nerdy.
27. #94 – Hair Type (Frizzy, Curly, etc.).
28. #97 – Braces.
29. #99 – Painted Nails.

# Romance (R)

1. #3 – Thick.
2. #8 – Chunky.
3. #13 – Loving.
4. #15 – Nosey.

5. #17 – Cowardly.
6. #19 – Flirtatious.
7. #22 – Painting/Drawing.
8. #27 – Singing.
9. #33 – British.
10. #37 – Australian.
11. #39 – Hispanic.
12. #41 – Piercings.
13. #45 – Implants.
14. #52 – Makeup Artist.
15. #53 – Author.
16. #55 – Fashion Designer.
17. #57 – Chef.
18. #59 – Bartender.
19. #61 – The Counselor – INFJ.
20. #67 – The Performer – ESFP.
21. #72 – Insecure.
22. #74 – Accusatory.
23. #78 – Controlling.
24. #81 – Goth.
25. #84 – Witchy.
26. #87 – Eclectic.
27. #90 – Elegant.
28. #91 – Freckles.
29. #95 – Stretch Marks.
30. #100 – Hairy.

## Horror (H)

1. #5 – Muscular.
2. #7 – Slender.
3. #13 – Loving.
4. #16 – Noisy.
5. #17 – Cowardly.
6. #20 – Shy.
7. #23 – Photography.
8. #25 – Cooking/Baking.
9. #30 – Vlogging.
10. #33 – British.

11. #37 – Australian.
12. #41 – Piercings.
13. #47 – Branding.
14. #48 – Scarification.
15. #52 – Makeup Artist.
16. #56 – Film Maker.
17. #57 – Chef.
18. #60 – Detective.
19. #62 – The Visionary – ENTP.
20. #67 – The Performer – ESFP.
21. #71 – Possessive.
22. #75 – Obsessive.
23. #80 – Mean-spirited.
24. #81 – Goth.
25. #85 – Vintage.
26. #88 – Retro.
27. #90 – Elegant.
28. #96 – Scars.
29. #100 – Hairy.

# Dystopian (D)

1. #4 – Short & Stumpy.
2. #10 – Bulky.
3. #12 – Sneaky.
4. #15 – Nosey.
5. #18 – Heroic.
6. #22 – Painting/Drawing.
7. #24 – Knitting.
8. #26 – Writing.
9. #29 – Traveling.
10. #32 – Jewish.
11. #34 – Irish.
12. #38 – Italian.
13. #40 – Asian.
14. #42 – Amputation.
15. #47 – Branding.
16. #51 – Cashier.

111

17. #53 – Author.
18. #57 – Chef.
19. #58 – Carpenter.
20. #64 – The Nurturer – ISFJ.
21. #68 – The Idealist – INFP.
22. #73 – Forgetful.
23. #74 – Accusatory.
24. #76 – Selfish.
25. #79 – Self-conscious.
26. #82 – Hipster.
27. #85 – Vintage.
28. #87 – Eclectic.
29. #90 – Elegant.
30. #93 – Tan Lines.
31. #96 – Scars.

## Slice of Life (SL)

1. #3 – Thick.
2. #11 – Naïve.
3. #14 – Magical.
4. #19 – Flirtatious.
5. #20 – Shy.
6. #21 – Violin.
7. #24 – Knitting.
8. #30 – Vlogging.
9. #31 – Native American.
10. #33 – British.
11. #34 – Irish.
12. #38 – Italian.
13. #44 – Botox.
14. #50 – Mechanical Implant.
15. #51 – Cashier.
16. #54 – EMT.
17. #55 – Fashion Designer.
18. #58 – Carpenter.
19. #64 – The Nurturer – ISFJ.
20. #68 – The Idealist – INFP.
21. #72 – Insecure.

22. #76 – Selfish.
23. #80 – Mean-spirited.
24. #82 – Hipster.
25. #85 – Vintage.
26. #88 – Retro.
27. #92 – Wrinkles.
28. #97 – Braces.

# Action & Adventure (AA)

1. #2 – Straight & Narrow.
2. #4 – Short & Stumpy.
3. #7 – Slender.
4. #11 – Naïve.
5. #14 – Magical.
6. #17 – Cowardly.
7. #18 – Heroic.
8. #26 – Writing.
9. #28 – Fishing.
10. #31 – Native American.
11. #34 – Irish.
12. #36 – African.
13. #39 – Hispanic.
14. #43 – Tattoos.
15. #48 – Scarification.
16. #53 – Author.
17. #54 – EMT.
18. #56 – Film Maker.
19. #60 – Detective.
20. #61 – The Counselor – INFJ.
21. #66 – The Doer – ESTP.
22. #69 – The Provider – ESFJ.
23. #73 – Forgetful.
24. #76 – Selfish.
25. #79 – Self-conscious.
26. #83 – Earthy.
27. #86 – Grunge.
28. #89 – Nerdy.
29. #91 – Freckles.

30. #94 – Hair Type (Frizzy, Curly, etc.).
31. #98 – Glasses.

# Mystery (M)

1.  #1 – Curvy.
2.  #6 – Well-toned.
3.  #9 – Broad.
4.  #12 – Sneaky.
5.  #13 – Loving.
6.  #15 – Nosey.
7.  #18 – Heroic.
8.  #21 – Violin.
9.  #28 – Fishing.
10. #32 – Jewish.
11. #35 – French.
12. #36 – African.
13. #37 – Australian.
14. #39 – Hispanic.
15. #40 – Asian.
16. #44 – Botox.
17. #50 – Mechanical Implant.
18. #52 – Makeup Artist.
19. #54 – EMT.
20. #56 – Film Maker.
21. #59 – Bartender.
22. #60 – Detective.
23. #63 – The Commander – ENTJ.
24. #65 – The Thinker – INTP.
25. #70 – The Champion – ENFP.
26. #71 – Possessive.
27. #73 – Forgetful.
28. #74 – Accusatory.
29. #78 – Controlling.
30. #80 – Mean-spirited.
31. #82 – Hipster.
32. #84 – Witchy.
33. #86 – Grunge.

34. #88 – Retro.
35. #92 – Wrinkles.
36. #98 – Glasses.

# Prompts by Medium

## Pencil (P)

1. #1 – Curvy.
2. #3 – Thick.
3. #6 – Well-toned.
4. #8 – Chunky.
5. #10 – Bulky.
6. #12 – Sneaky.
7. #15 – Nosey.
8. #17 – Cowardly.
9. #19 – Flirtatious.
10. #23 – Photography.
11. #25 – Cooking/Baking.
12. #27 – Singing.
13. #29 – Traveling.
14. #32 – Jewish.
15. #34 – Irish.
16. #37 – Australian.
17. #38 – Italian.
18. #41 – Piercings.
19. #43 – Tattoos.
20. #45 – Implants.
21. #47 – Branding.
22. #50 – Mechanical Implant.
23. #52 – Makeup Artist.
24. #54 – EMT.
25. #56 – Film Maker.
26. #59 – Bartender.
27. #61 – The Counselor – INFJ.
28. #64 – The Nurturer – ISFJ.
29. #66 – The Doer – ESTP.
30. #70 – The Champion – ENFP.
31. #71 – Possessive.
32. #74 – Accusatory.
33. #78 – Controlling.
34. #81 – Goth.
35. #84 – Witchy.

36. #87 – Eclectic.
37. #89 – Nerdy.
38. #91 – Freckles.
39. #94 – Hair Type (Frizzy, Curly, etc.).
40. #97 – Braces.
41. #100 – Hairy.

# Marker (M)

1. #2 – Straight & Narrow.
2. #4 – Short & Stumpy.
3. #7 – Slender.
4. #9 – Broad.
5. #11 – Naïve.
6. #14 – Magical.
7. #15 – Nosey.
8. #19 – Flirtatious.
9. #21 – Violin.
10. #23 – Photography.
11. #26 – Writing.
12. #28 – Fishing.
13. #30 – Vlogging.
14. #31 – Native American.
15. #34 – Irish.
16. #36 – African.
17. #39 – Hispanic.
18. #43 – Tattoos.
19. #46 – Fantasy. (Pointed Ears, Fangs, etc.)
20. #48 – Scarification.
21. #51 – Cashier.
22. #54 – EMT.
23. #57 – Chef.
24. #60 – Detective.
25. #62 – The Visionary – ENTP.
26. #65 – The Thinker – INTP.
27. #67 – The Performer – ESFP.
28. #69 – The Provider – ESFJ.
29. #71 – Possessive.

30. #75 – Obsessive.
31. #79 – Self-conscious.
32. #83 – Earthy.
33. #85 – Vintage.
34. #88 – Retro.
35. #93 – Tan Lines.
36. #96 – Scars.
37. #98 – Glasses.

# Ink (I)

1. #3 – Thick.
2. #5 – Muscular.
3. #7 – Slender.
4. #10 – Bulky.
5. #11 – Naïve.
6. #13 – Loving.
7. #16 – Noisy.
8. #19 – Flirtatious.
9. #21 – Violin.
10. #24 – Knitting.
11. #26 – Writing.
12. #29 – Traveling.
13. #32 – Jewish.
14. #36 – African.
15. #40 – Asian.
16. #42 – Amputation.
17. #44 – Botox.
18. #47 – Branding.
19. #49 – Robotic Limb.
20. #51 – Cashier.
21. #53 – Author.
22. #56 – Film Maker
23. #58 – Carpenter.
24. #62 – The Visionary – ENTP.
25. #65 – The Thinker – INTP.
26. #68 – The Idealist – INFP.
27. #72 – Insecure.
28. #74 – Accusatory.

29. #78 – Controlling.
30. #80 – Mean-spirited.
31. #82 – Hipster.
32. #85 – Vintage.
33. #88 – Retro.
34. #90 – Elegant.
35. #92 – Wrinkles.
36. #94 – Hair Type (Frizzy, Curly, etc.).
37. #96 – Scars.
38. #99 – Painted Nails.

# Crayon (C)

1. #3 – Thick.
2. #4 – Short & Stumpy.
3. #7 – Slender.
4. #13 – Loving.
5. #17 – Cowardly.
6. #22 – Painting/Drawing.
7. #24 – Knitting.
8. #27 – Singing.
9. #30 – Vlogging.
10. #33 – British.
11. #37 – Australian.
12. #39 – Hispanic.
13. #41 – Piercings.
14. #44 – Botox.
15. #47 – Branding.
16. #49 – Robotic Limb.
17. #52 – Makeup Artist.
18. #56 – Film Maker.
19. #59 – Bartender.
20. #62 – The Visionary – ENTP.
21. #64 – The Nurturer – ISFJ.
22. #67 – The Performer – ESFP.
23. #69 – The Provider – ESFJ.
24. #73 – Forgetful.
25. #76 – Selfish.

26. #79 – Self-conscious.
27. #83 – Earthy.
28. #86 – Grunge.
29. #89 – Nerdy.
30. #91 – Freckles.
31. #95 – Stretch Marks.
32. #97 – Braces.
33. #100   Hairy.

# Gouache (G)

1.  #2 – Straight & Narrow.
2.  #6 – Well-toned.
3.  #9 – Broad.
4.  #12 – Sneaky.
5.  #14 – Magical.
6.  //17 – Cowardly.
7.  #20 – Shy.
8.  #22 – Painting/Drawing.
9.  #26 – Writing.
10. #28 – Fishing.
11. #33 – British.
12. #35 – French.
13. #37 – Australian.
14. #40 – Asian.
15. #41 – Piercings.
16. #44 – Botox.
17. #46 – Fantasy. (Pointed Ears, Fangs, etc.)
18. #50 – Mechanical Implant.
19. #52 – Makeup Artist.
20. #55 – Fashion Designer.
21. #58 – Carpenter.
22. #60 – Detective.
23. #63 – The Commander – ENTJ.
24. #65 – The Thinker – INTP.
25. #68 – The Idealist – INFP.
26. #70 – The Champion – ENFP.
27. #71 – Possessive.

121

28. #73 – Forgetful.
29. #76 – Selfish.
30. #80 – Mean-spirited.
31. #81 – Goth.
32. #84 – Witchy.
33. #86 – Grunge.
34. #89 – Nerdy.
35. #92 – Wrinkles.
36. #93 – Tan Lines.
37. #95 – Stretch Marks.
38. #98 – Glasses.

# Acrylic Paint (AP)

1. #1 – Curvy.
2. #5 – Muscular.
3. #9 – Broad.
4. #12 – Sneaky.
5. #15 – Nosey.
6. #18 – Heroic.
7. #20 – Shy.
8. #22 – Painting/Drawing.
9. #27 – Singing.
10. #30 – Vlogging.
11. #32 – Jewish.
12. #34 – Irish.
13. #36 – African.
14. #39 – Hispanic.
15. #42 – Amputation.
16. #46 – Fantasy. (Pointed Ears, Fangs, etc.)
17. #49 – Robotic Limb.
18. #50 – Mechanical Implant.
19. #53 – Author.
20. #55 – Fashion Designer.
21. #58 – Carpenter.
22. #61 – The Counselor – INFJ.
23. #64 – The Nurturer – ISFJ.
24. #67 – The Performer – ESFP.

25. #70 – The Champion – ENFP.
26. #72 – Insecure.
27. #75 – Obsessive.
28. #78 – Controlling.
29. #81 – Goth.
30. #83 – Earthy.
31. #86 – Grunge.
32. #88 – Retro.
33. #92 – Wrinkles.
34. #95 – Stretch Marks.
35. #98 – Glasses.
36. #100 – Hairy.

## Color Pencil (CP)

1. #2 – Straight & Narrow.
2. #5 – Muscular.
3. #8 – Chunky.
4. #10 – Bulky.
5. #11 – Naïve.
6. #14 – Magical.
7. #16 – Noisy.
8. #18 – Heroic.
9. #21 – Violin.
10. #24 – Knitting.
11. #25 – Cooking/Baking.
12. #29 – Traveling.
13. #31 – Native American.
14. #33 – British.
15. #35 – French.
16. #38 – Italian.
17. #40 – Asian.
18. #43 – Tattoos.
19. #45 – Implants.
20. #48 – Scarification.
21. #51 – Cashier.
22. #54 – EMT.
23. #57 – Chef.

24. #60 – Detective.
25. #63 – The Commander – ENTJ.
26. #66 – The Doer – ESTP.
27. #68 – The Idealist – INFP.
28. #73 – Forgetful.
29. #75 – Obsessive.
30. #79 – Self-conscious.
31. #82 – Hipster.
32. #85 – Vintage.
33. #87 – Eclectic.
34. #90 – Elegant.
35. #93 – Tan Lines.
36. #94 – Hair Type (Frizzy, Curly, etc.).
37. #97 – Braces.
38. #99 – Painted Nails.

# Watercolor (W)

1. #1 – Curvy.
2. #4 – Short & Stumpy.
3. #6 – Well-toned.
4. #8 – Chunky.
5. #13 – Loving.
6. #16 – Noisy.
7. #18 – Heroic.
8. #20 – Shy.
9. #23 – Photography.
10. #25 – Cooking/Baking.
11. #28 – Fishing.
12. #31 – Native American.
13. #35 – French.
14. #38 – Italian.
15. #42 – Amputation.
16. #45 – Implants.
17. #48 – Scarification.
18. #53 – Author.
19. #55 – Fashion Designer.
20. #57 – Chef.

21. #59 – Bartender.
22. #61 – The Counselor – INFJ.
23. #63 – The Commander – ENTJ.
24. #66 – The Doer – ESTP.
25. #69 – The Provider – ESFJ.
26. #72 – Insecure.
27. #74 – Accusatory.
28. #76 – Sclfish.
29. #80 – Mean-spirited.
30. #82 – Hipster.
31. #84 – Witchy.
32. #87 – Eclectic.
33. #90 – Elegant.
34. #91 – Freckles.
35. #96 – Scars.
36. #99 – Painted Nails.

# Writing Exercises

1. Write about the transition of weight gain/loss.
2. Write a character with a split personality – and explore the characteristics of all of them.
3. Write out your process for partaking in your favorite hobby – in story-format.
4. Conduct an interview with someone of a different race and/or ethnicity.
5. Write about someone's experience getting something modified.
6. Write about a character's preparation process for an interview.
7. Write a character with a personality that you love.
8. Write a character with three traits that you hate.
9. Write about a day in the life of a character with an aesthetic that you idolize.
10. Write about a detective who is looking for someone with specific features.

# Drawing Exercises

1. Draw 10 different body types in a line-up.
2. Draw 10 different facial expressions that are tied to different characteristics.
3. Draw a collection of supplies used for your hobby.
4. Draw a collection of things associated with a culture.
5. Draw a group of people with different body modifications.
6. Draw 10 different types of work uniforms.
7. Draw the same character 10 times – each with a different personality.
8. Draw an object that relates to one of the traits listed in this chapter.
    a. Ex: Forgetful – Scattered sticky notes.
9. Draw a collection of items that relate to one of the listed aesthetics.
10. Draw a character with 5 features you admire.

# Thank You!

That's all for now! We hope you had fun exploring your creative side! If you did, please considering leaving us a review. We'd really appreciate it!

You can come back next year for our 2021 edition and do a whole new set of prompts, and a new set of exercises.

But in the meantime, if you're looking for something to keep you busy, you can try our other prompt books:

- 365 Writing Prompts.
- 365 Drawing Prompts.
- 100 Quote Prompts.
- And more!

And if you're looking for something fun to read to give you some inspiration, check out our fiction books and comics!

For more information, check out our website, www.TCStudiosHQ.com.

www.ingramcontent.com/pod-product-compliance
Lightning Source LLC
Chambersburg PA
CBHW081728220526
45468CB00008B/2017